MW01577047

This journal belongs to:

Made in the USA
Monee, IL
16 December 2019

18802123R00061